AFTERMATH

poems

The events described in this book represent the recollection of the author as she experienced them.

Editing: Kelsey Sipple
Cover design: Angelicque Roa
Cover art: Kelsey Sipple

ISBN (paperback): 979-8991853040
ISBN (ebook): 979-8991853057

First Edition
Published by Girl Noise Press
girlnoise.press

AFTERMATH

poems by catherine broadwall

GIRL NOISE

Contents

Part Three
PRISM

For anyone who has had to reinvent themselves.

Part One
CALDERA

Landing

Outside the airplane window, sun cuffs
the shoulders of the frozen mountain range,
and my life as I knew it is over.

The Coke is diluted with melted ice
above pastures and cities where
people fret and dream. I stir it:

a fizzing, auburn floe.
I echo this, too — inside my chest,
a whirlpool. A cycloning of livestock.

And still, despite this, I would not
revise my love. I would rather
be the cattle spinning madly in a storm.

I would rather be the barn
than the wind that breaks the barn.
Rather be the fish than the knife

that guts the fish. Rather be the mug
than the floor that cracks the mug,
rather be the field

than the flame that scars the field.
I would rather be the dead star
than the vacuum.

I would rather these things not happen
at all. But drink your dregs now;
we are scraping the runway.

Sundown

Dreamt I sat in a stalled car out on a tundra,
canvas-white. The sun swam low, a goldfish
chasing two lovers, red and indigo clouds.

My mittened hand held a phone, and a woman
spoke into my ear. She was selling me something
that had to do with the house you and I once shared.

Yes, I told her. *I lived there once.* Ice, by now,
was walking up the windows with clawed reptile
prints. The sky was a marble, fragile and

condensed. My heart was like this too as the
woman tried to pitch me insurance I no longer
need. The sun had gone to bed with the lavender

clouds. Darkness spread like a duvet. I stayed
on the phone. I had affection for the woman. I was
lonely and her voice seemed so persuasive. I liked

to hear her talk. I asked about the pros and cons,
the silver and platinum tiers. She chatted about
the coverage, promising this was the policy to end

all policies, the one with the best defense. I sat there,
a dot on the iceberg all night. And though I may not
have been loved, I was loveable. This much I know.

Origin Story of the Oracle

A ghost sits in the corner of the party.
You try not to look at her, avoid her
all night. Talk to every other guest,
their froth-filled cups bright red.

She finds you in the bathroom, though.
You know how it is: you go to fix
your lipstick, and suddenly the last
person in the world you want to see

stands beside you in the dive bar mirror.
Your faux-satin dress won't protect you
from this. Nothing from the sale rack can.
Though, for that matter, nothing designer

would have preserved you either.
The ghost hovers over to you, not even
pulling out a customary compact
to reapply her blush. She is all business

tonight, her eyes pleading inkwells
overfilled with ink. You glower when
she puts her arms around you. Traces
the circle of your shoulder. Whispers

her apologies, meeting your eyes in the
mirror, never turning to face you.
Never connecting in the real world,
only in this neutral glass, the realm

of unsaid truce. The lights flicker off,
and with that, she is gone. You find you
can conjure small flames in your palms,
just bright enough to divine by.

Falling Three Ways

goodbye to

                    the girl with

tombstone eyes and

              hair down to her waist, whose

aubergine nails that scrape the

                porcelain teacup of honey

release,

                    abruptly

announcing, falling —— *I am a shattered star that*

                    continues to plummet, but

burrows, upon its descent to the earth; a seed

                    does not extinguish

Alchemy

Oceanic gargoyle perched at the spraying
bow of the cumulous ferry. Claws in pockets

chip red sparkle. Home-dyed hair streams
violet. Violent. Destinations wait like strangers'

mouths on dark dancefloors. Say *banality*; she'll tell
you about the crisp letter from the Peace Corps:

Too many issues with food, its crease snapped. It's true
she's lost too many gold rings, forgotten in public rest

stalls. A purging, an attempted exorcism. A rejection
of the world. Say *acuity*; she'll tell you about the nice

lady therapist who told her to give up: *You can't
get milk from the butcher,* she tsked. A gory metaphor

for the girl who refused to *kill two birds with one stone,*
rearranging letters to *feed two birds with one seed.* A bleeding

heart as red as the lipstick she flaunts in airports, hoping
and dreading, re-hoping and re-dreading that someone

will admonish or kiss her. She cannot always tell which.
Say *audacity*; she'll tell you about how the ferry feels

symbolic. *You have to face forward, never backward. That's not
the way you're going.* These arbitrary icepicks we throw at the

steep, the glacial blue of the world. How she stands
at the bow and breathes in the salt, the lashing sideways

bluster. How this is the ultimate exorcist's act —
inhaling the broken invisible. Holding it in

one's gargoyle chest. Then spouting it
back out as flame.

Murals

In the city so hot, the tops of your feet burn in minutes — the city where you slide into beanstalks of shade cast by telephone poles while waiting for crosswalk lights to change — you guide a group of children through a weeklong summer camp. This is an art camp, and the students look to you with bright anticipation if they are young, reserved hope if they are older. They want to see what you will do.

Always, you show them watercolors, the way the paint changes if you apply it to dry paper versus wet. You show them how applying wet paint to wet paper causes it to bleed and run into rivulets you couldn't have made on your own. The way the paint develops its own wildness. They practice this, making foxes with galaxies for eyes and sandcastles that reach toward the sky like hands.

Always, taking care that each plastic thermos is filled with cool water and each neon backpack is secure, you wind them through the blazing city until you reach the outdoor gallery of transient murals. They span for blocks, mermaids and butterflies rising up alongside dumpsters and fire hydrants, existing together in a tenuous ecosystem.

The paintings change annually, except for a few permanent ones made from shattered mirrors. The artists who come and refresh the walls create all manner of things — sometimes haunting, sometimes tranquil. A monstrous green face with long, jagged teeth leers out from one shadowed corner. A pig soaring skyward with the aid of a balloon decorates the side of a café.

You do not know it yet, but soon, you will shelter inside your home for months, and all the summer camps will be canceled. You do not know it yet, but soon, someone will tell you that you add nothing to the world, that you only take, and you will flee this city like a startled tumbleweed, supernova arrhythmia hammering your chest. You will question the words' truth for years.

For now, though, you are here, hand shielding your eyes from the sun as you smile at the campers. You wander the alleys as the kids take gulps from bottles, tap their notebooks with their pencils. *Choose an image,* you tell them, *and write in its voice. Who are you today? Which one speaks to you?* You gaze around at ghosts, roaring serpents, praying angels. *Let them tell you what they have to say.*

Hematite Heart

Once, my godmother gave me a box of hearts
that could hang from chains as pendants.

Each one made of different stone: agate,
jasper, quartz. *What heart will I wake*

up with today? I wonder, an adult now,
laced with flecks of pain. Glinting with veins

marbled with memory. One of the stone hearts
was hematite: a glossy, silver substance

polished as battle armor, heavy as a mace
laid on the ground. I wore this, sometimes,

on difficult days: as a girl, as a teen, as a woman
brimmed with silence, or, other days,

with words. What heart will I wake up
with today? The turbulent ocean of lapis lazuli?

The sunrise blush of carnelian? Or will it be
hematite, the ore that crouches like a dumbbell

in the hutch of my chest? Forgive me, world. This
is all I can be: traipsing through the night

like a Maypole drenched with ribbons, gazing at the
gloaming from this rock where I perch, encircled by

spiraling stream. Breathing in the wind, feeling barely
embodied, anchored by the thrum behind my ribs.

Apology

I am so sorry.

I will always be the girl
with a little bit of lemon cake
batter on her shiny new keyboard.
Always be the girl with the blue hair
dye and a pair of wadded gloves
beneath the bathroom sink.
Most likely, the hair dye will stain
some ceramic. The tub, perhaps.
The shower wall. I will always use lip
balm instead of lipstick. Always
have mud stains on my thick boots.
A transportation deviant, too scared
to drive, I will always be trudging
through the slush to the bus,
where I will brood, most likely,
or cry over shot wolves. I will always
be crying for this species
or that. Always glowering
at ugly power. When I meet you
on dates, or for coffee, or for
readings, I will always be part
animal, part gale.

Ecology

Having trained myself on poison,
the melon tastes especially sweet,

pinned with bright tines to the
good dishes. Soft fruit oozing

its creamsicle juice. Sky that
reflects in its puddle.

Everything sugared and miracle
light. Wind hardly rattling

the table. I want to be a wife.
I want to be an artist. I hope

these impulses
are not in contradiction,

will not quarrel like
territorial foxes

chancing an encounter
in a wood.

To wife: to comb out
the snarls of life (?). To write:

to roll down a grass hill (?).
I want to be smooth. I want

to be rough. I want to be
moonlight and shelter.

And what is the natural enemy of
the woman who wants to do both?

My heart pumps blood into
my seesaw head

until all of my hair
is fire-red.

Impasse

When we finally painted the bedroom turquoise, it felt like coming home. I dreamt of it for years: a room I could swim in. A waterfall of blue. Though we lived in a desert state, in ochre and bronze, I came from a coastal town. Just the smell of saltwater sets off symphonies in my veins. Pavlovian, synesthetic reaction. The sea sounds to me like a violin note: a clear, crisp rind on the horizon. Linear, a pane of glass, scooched against the sky. The gray of it, the cobalt ribbon gleaming. When I entered the room then, I thought, *Barnacles, seagulls. Red kelp and hermit crabs' scuttle.* I swam there. I swam through the cavern of green. My forked, fanned tail brushed the marble prince's hip. His stone fingers stroked the thrumming gills on my left cheek. The moon a huge sand dollar, rising.

Burnout

I want to stare for a very long time
in a mirror and comb my hair out.

Want to comb my hair out with
seashell teeth and watch my skin

turn green. The aquamarine
of the painted walls tinting my cheeks,

a billowing blush. Want to pull
barnacles from my hair and set

them on the bureau. String them on
a length of lace. Wear it around

my throat. I want to converse
with the moon in moonlight,

whisper cups of silver. Stroll
barefoot through fields

of buckwheat. Vanish
with the night.

I want it to be all right to be
the strange, shifting creature

I am. Somewhere far
from gears and clocks.

With a rustle of feathers,
I'd go.

Oyster's Clutch

You are the grit,
the jagged speck embedded

between silver folds of memory
and the mantle of dispassion.

Gut of heart and hourglass eye
cannot dislodge the wound.

The splinter of beach glosses to luster,
a small and white-knuckled ravaging ball.

With two prying fingers I unhinge the shell
and rob the furtive chamber of its oceanic sore.

I string them on a rosary, these wretched gorgeous pearls,
a collar of stars that glows like wet teeth

in lean hands ribboned with teal.
I thumb the touchstones faded and mutter fevered prayers,

circle coral mandalas, and serenade slow fins.
Specter of salt, anguish of time,

here in the sea belly church you
are transcended.

Although you have haunted
this oyster mind for years,

you are now a muted pebble
in the graveyard of dark dreams —

meditative, harmless, a talisman rent
by searching nimble fingers

from obsession's clenched bone jaw.

Corn Maze

Each autumn, I begged to be taken
to the country fair. A way to stave off
silence, if only for a day. Grudgingly,
he'd drive me there, allotting himself

a small smile, perhaps, as I *ooh*ed over cider,
*aah*ed over gourds. I dragged him through
the inflatable monster. We'd spin around in
its soft esophagus. Me squealing

and flinching as the red pulsed dark
and harpsichords played from boomboxes.
I performed emotion like a drowning rat,
paddling hard enough to try to save us both.

Knowing full well it was in vain. It was always
something haunted with him — in Paris,
place known as the City of Love,
his only request was the skull-lined catacombs.

I clutched his sleeve in the deep.
I clutch his sleeve, now, as we travel
the corn maze, tall stalks swaying as the
orange sun sinks and twilight seeps into

the shadows of his hair. I had wanted to wing it,
to navigate by luck, by trial and error, with infinite
patience. Of course, this had me running toward
innumerable dead ends. So he placed his hand

against the left wall, fingertips grazing the desiccated
cobs. Even now, as air grows cold and wind
picks up, it is a long way back from the center.
I begin to worry as stars blink on: at 10 PM,

they let the zombie farmers out into the maze,
and it will be much harder after that. I trusted
him, and he never looked at me, those times.
Following him was a labyrinth. I had been willing

to wander and explore. He was only after
the exit. I hear a crunch and rustling, a wailing
moan go up, as shapes slip by in my periphery.
Neither chance nor strategy can rescue us now.

Something has come for the harvest.

Fairytale Adjacent

A pale moon lodged in my throat,
wedge round and white as an apple.

I comb my hair out — once, twice —
and hope, like Snow White, it won't

venom me dead. Streetlamps are
flickering above suburban roses.

I stare down my own reflection.
Searching for what, I can't say.

Can I even still dream, now? Even
still want? After all that *unreeling*?

After the language I honed to speak
to you was stuffed like a sock

down a hole? In the mirror, I spy
eyeliner montages. Each morning,

I layer it on. Each night, wash it off.
Each day, I prepare my neck

for the grasping touch of the world.
Like smoke rings I choke through.

Each evening, I cut up apples, searching,
searching in the heartwood seeds.

I suppose I'll know it when I see it:
the beautiful thing, the fairest, that

will make me look up
and gasp.

After Bluebeard

Consider, for a moment, the wife of Bluebeard:

the last wife,

      I mean.   The one who lives.

Consider what she might say,   could she speak.

      What support groups

she might seek.   Imagine her

logging onto Zoom with shaking hands,

watching her own face flicker on the screen

      alongside all those boxed-in others.

*

      The first night I saw him

      put down more

than a twelve-pack,   I swear,

his lips turned blue.   An icy kind of purple

that startled.   I was twenty.

An omen,   those lavender lips.

Blue lips, Blue beard. I can't say I was not warned.

Blue lips, Blue beard. I was

warned.

*

Imagine how she must have arrived on tiptoe

at the castle, the lady

in white. Her gown barely making

a sound upon the earth. Its stone

presence made her

        fall silent.

Something about her new home seeming ominous,

   something like a shadow

on the face of the moon that scuttled,

that skittered away.

Something lurking in the corner of her eye,

  simmering just out of view.

*

I quickly discovered   my new roommates

        were bottles in every shade of glass.

Green, clear, amber: they glittered on the table,

they glittered in the full recycling bin.

They glittered   like quiet, dull teeth.

Clear, amber, green: their mouths open, empty.

Their contents swimming,   metabolizing,

in his belly as the sun crept toward noon.

        Sometimes I would blow across them,

                sending flute song   to only

my own hungry ears.   He slept   and slept

as the sun rose higher,

        the glass teeth closing   in.

Amber, green, clear: sometimes broken,

sometimes hurtled   at parties   where I would

fall silent.

*

Imagine her flowing   about her new home,   always

        aware of his watching.

How he eyed her with contempt

            as she played her piano,   or danced

(depending on which version you are reading —

often, though,   she is an artist).

Imagine him handing off the key ring one day,

making a grand exit with a bottle in hand.

        Use any key except that, he might say,

then stumble to an Uber with a wide sneer.

Imagine her wanting   and not wanting   to know.

        Wanting and unwanting

the answer.

Imagine her fingering   the small gold key

that flashes in the light like her gold ring.

*

        Imagine me calling   after stumbling upon

forbidden knowledge,

my hands, my arms shaking.   Every   part of me

shaking.

Imagine me saying, *I need*   *the truth.*   *Did you do*

that thing   *you promised*

you didn't?   *That thing you promised*   *you didn't do*

for years?   *Then lie?*   *Then lie?*

Then lie?

*

Imagine what the girl must   have thought,   looking in

that   forbidden   room.

Bluebeard's murdered past wives,   throats closed,

so silent.   Imagine

how her mind   must have tripped for a moment,

trying to push them away.

And then   imagine   what else

she must have felt.

Revulsion. Terror.   Her shaking   hands.

            Dropping

the key   in the blood.

*

            You cannot unknow, thinks the girl in the story.

            You cannot unknow, says the voice in my head

as I stare   at the phone screen,   having hung up.

            The silence like dull, wet teeth.

*

Imagine the rage that Bluebeard brings down,

having had   his secret   uncovered.

            Imagine how he bellows and storms the marble halls.

            Imagine how she cowers,

eyes pooling.   As if she is the one

who has whirlwinded lives

as casually as pinching out a candle.   *Yes,*

she seems to say   with her wringing of hands.

Yes, it is I   *who have trespassed.*

*

          Yes, I seem to say   in my many Zoom calls,

          support groups,   my many

relinquishments.   *Yes, it is I*   *who have failed so greatly.*

                    I eat sins   as eagerly

as if they are cupcakes.

I lick the whipped cream from my hands.

*

Imagine the girl on the chopping block,

weeping,   saying,   *Yes.*

Yes, it is I   *who have done something wrong. I'm sorry.   I'm so,*

so sorry.

Depending on which version of the story you are reading,

this is the moment where her brothers intervene,

or her mother: they burst in,
swords blazing.   Vanquishing

Bluebeard and saving the girl

who is somehow   still   stammering, *Yes.*

*

Depending on which version of the story you are reading,

          sometimes the key is stained, but also   the girl.

          A mark

appears on her body.   No soap   will scrub it

     away.   For me,

no mark,   but a stain nonetheless:

I will never   have not

wept alone on the wedding night

seeing how far I had strayed   from myself.

I will never   not   have winced at the sound

of a bottle cap leaving   its neck.

Never again   will I never have buried

a ring at the center of the island   where we met.

Never will I not have lowered to my knees

and dug in the ivy in the rain.

This is the stain   I am left with.   It marks not my body,

          but this portion of the thread

I use   to weave   my life.

Never again will I not have to point and say,

              Here is where I went off course.

*

And yet, I want to write a new story for the maiden,

      one where she doesn't whisper, *Yes.*

I want to take her cold hands,

raise her head from the block,   help her   to her feet.

I want to turn back pages   to the scene

where her husband   glowers at her over the key.

I want to cheer   as she glares right back   and says,

No,   *I'm not the one at fault here.*

*

In many versions of the story,   the girl remarries.

Imagine: a fairy tale

allowing second marriage.

Allowing a "stained" girl to thrive.

The moral   not being   *Curiosity kills,*   but

          You can shapeshift and thrive.

You need not walk with your head hung low, hands wringing.

Look up. Look forward.

Look at all this old world offers you.

I want to write a story where the maiden and her new love

          wander in fields,   eat honey.

I want to write a story of gentleness for her. I want this to be

          permitted.

To spin new thread with the memories of new love,

          for they have stained my life too:

never again   will I never have thrilled at

     the sight of my new love

throwing back his head   and laughing as we

make the same joke at the same time.

Never will I ever   not feel the mark

of my own nails digging   into my palm,

so badly   did I want   to reach for him.

          Never will I ever

not have felt my heart surge   as he reached out

          for me.

*

Imagine a girl walking over smashed bottles,

          out of a castle made of glass.

Imagine the moat and its froth of hops scent.   Imagine

the drawbridge coming down.

The girl holds a key so red,   it glows like sunrise.

It reliquefies   in the smelter of her grip.

And when her palm opens, the burning metal morphs

          to the curved spine of a harp.

Bright threads form the strings.   Memories sourced

from her head in shades of crimson,

sapphire, glinting gold.   As she begins to strum them,

a roar might go up from the castle,

an insult, a slurred bark.   But she will keep walking,

          crack the sun like a yolk

if she has to, to suck out its goodness.

          Such is her desperation; such is her resolve.

          To scrape a little pleasure from this life.

And after all that,   as wind sweeps the field,

mightn't she like   to change her ending?

Mightn't she like   to change it?

Part Two
SHAPESHIFTER

Shears

In 2004, a sheep named Shrek, who had wandered from his flock in New Zealand and lived in a cave for six years, was discovered. When the immense fleece he had grown was shorn, it was said to produce enough material for twenty coats. A few months later, he was shorn again on an iceberg that floated past the coast of the country.

The man who found him said
he looked like a Biblical creature —
Shrek the sheep, overgrown
with wool. A full sixty pounds of it,
puffed across his body. Shrek
from the German *schreck*: terror.

What would you do
if fear came to you like this?
Lumbering, primordial, crushed
beneath the bulk of its own
bounty — of what it had made?
Elusive as a feather, chthonic
as a board: *one, two, three* — !

Does that slumber party game
ever actually work? Does it lift
trancing girls in their nightgowns?
If fear came to me, I would take
it to the iceberg, the way they
did with Shrek: a spectacle.

I would fasten small crampons
onto its hooves. Plant my own
feet in the blue cold. Would cut

away clusters from those sunstruck
eyes. And when I was finished,
what a gown I would have. Twenty
nightgowns to gallop, to rise in.

Home Again

That first bus ride after moving
back home, I cooed over
everything, enraptured.

The bricks of the station
seemed folkloric, enchanting.
Oceanic firs blurring by windows

a symphony of light.
Even the pigeons seemed elegant,
profound. This is what comes

from loving a place: you find
beauty everywhere.

Darling

My friend gives me an orchid
the care tag calls Your Darling.
Water Your Darling once a week:
two tablespoons, lukewarm.
Your Darling enjoys the sunlight.
But not too much. Just enough.

I am not a common keeper
of plants, having killed a number
of violets, amaryllis. Knocked over
a succulent, watched its earth scatter
across the waxed hardwood.

I want to keep My Darling alive,
want to be someone's Darling
kept in a ray of sunlight, *not*
too much. I think of the ways
we reveal ourselves: the quirks
that sparkle with charm. My friend
with the binder of catalogued teas.
My friend with the necklace of
fruit. My friend with the collages
of tigers and seals. Their dimpled,
half-moon grins.

When someone calls you worthless,
you might question these things
in yourself. *What exactly*
was worthless? You might look
at the glass mermaid,
the anime T-shirt,
and wonder, *Was it*

this? The things you find
darling about yourself — deemed
worthless. Deemed having-no-worth.

Once, in a computer game, the goal
was to woo a lover, get them to marry
your avatar. You had to build up
a slate of heart points. You had to fill up
their heart gauge. My digital wife
and I met on a dancefloor, so after
we wed, I always took her dancing.
I wanted to keep her heart full.

When I told this to the man
I was seeing at the time, he said,
It doesn't matter. It can empty.
They won't leave. God sends
signs to those who listen.

My Darling, My Darling,
I will always cherish
your binder of tea flavors.
Your necklace of fruit.
Will never find worthless
your wild creations. Will
always see the moon in your
half-smile. *Water Your Darling*
weekly, daily, hourly if you can.
Water Your Darling, since
the heart is a pie near a
mountain of ravenous ants.
The heart a gauge nibbled away.

My Darling, I will never let you
erode. I promise I will always
read your care tag. Your charms

will never be lost on me. Cross my
heart: I will always bloom awe.

Imagine

We sit overlooking the water,
share rice with a takeout spoon.

Salt flicks the air and young gulls
screech and grass submits to wind.

I am so happy, I think I have died.
I mean, literally, it crosses my mind:

Maybe I have died. Seeing you again
after so long. Seeing how our faces

change in photos. Me, with my glasses
now. You with your long hair. And

what is not pictured: the luggage carts
of pain. The turquoise waves

are glittering. The seashells
fresh and bright.

Imagine, you sometimes say. *Imagine
not loving the ocean.* You shake your head

in pity. *Imagine not loving the breeze.*
Imagine a happiness so abounding,

you have to scan your memory
for traces of demise. Imagine

what must have preceded this.
A life so laced with ache.

Am I alive?
The salt. The wind.

The takeout spoon
between us.

Your fingers gently
brushing mine.

Am I alive?
You are.

egg tarts

what would my life be
without this anxiety?

I want to know the true
face of joy. & it's here,

I think, in the egg tarts
we rise early for, running

to the bakery & pointing
at the case. the gold cream

& crisp crust &
your face smiling —

a crumb on your cheek,
the same spot where

your dad gets one,
the spot your mom brushes

the way that I now do.
your hair in the night

smelling like my rose shampoo,
the way the air against

my throat is breath,
not a fan. they say nothing

is permanent. I know.
I know. but let me

snatch this gleam back
from the void.

let the egg tarts runneth
over. soften. soften.

let the captured birds
fly out to sea.

Making Luck

Stirred the pumpkin bread in a hurry,
got a bite of salt. Days trod on and I try
to be a hopeful self, a sylph. A fox
with her nose to the wind instead of
scratching at the dirt. Inhaling
futures, fields. Heart, help me track
the wildflowers bursting into brightness.
Help me chase the lightning bugs that glimmer
by the pier. The heart is a sturdy compass
that somebody dropped on the stairs.
The heart is a torch that got rained on
but sputters anyway. I ate the bread
despite its tantrum. Ate it, salt and all.

Offering

I see you there, self, cursing
the rain, trudging your way uphill.
Your hat is too thin, your
backpack too heavy, and why
the damn bus didn't come,
I don't know. I don't know.
I don't know why people break
stained glass windows with rocks,
pull sleeping pet tails. I don't
know why he said those things,
made you feel diffuse as a cloud.
Maybe it's why that scorpion
in the fable stings the frog. Why
It's in my nature is what the creature
sings as both begin to drown.
My God, is it difficult to keep
an open heart, to ferry the cobwebs
away. But look, the bouquet
of the woman in front of you —
trudging up the same hill — has let
loose a bloom. Look, you're running
after her — the rain, it seems,
is everywhere — she smiles.
She says, *You can keep it.*

Almost a Miracle

The home I wake in is the home I've always
wanted, being that you are here. I groggily

stir coffee, wear your pajama bottoms,
walk past the photograph of us as kids.

The tree out our window: a kaleidoscope
of beauty, obscuring the parking lot, the bins

overflowing with trash. If you squint and tilt
your head, it is almost perfect. If you let yourself go

dizzy, you can almost ignore
the desiccated rat on the morning footpath.

Bless the cockroaches who pass us by —
the inspector says it is almost a miracle

we haven't seen one in our unit. Bless their
shells and mini legs that stay on their side

of the wavering line between nature and
whatever this is. The woman at the conference

says we *are* nature, even in this
taupe cracked-paint complex. Birds

come and sit in the branches of the tree,
bounce on its cushy moss coat. Now

and then, squirrels come and dangle, bellies
so close, I could almost reach out and

scritch them. From what I can tell, ours is
the only unit that comes with this

simple perk. We are here, and you love me, and
we are nature, and yes, this is my life.

The gold leaves, the dead rat, and your
pajama bottoms. Yes. I shall call this my life.

Joy Spell

The grimoires all say
language and intention
form a simple magic.

I have cast love spells.
Wish spells. Burnt candles
to the hilt. Conjured

this and that, gratefully.
But here in the kitchen,
as honey drips down

our chins and we laugh,
a sound like rhinestones,
I issue a joy spell.

The language
our laughter. The honey
our hot wax, our seal.

Solstice

When the online witch says, *Drink the salt,*
perhaps what she means is to winter inside
the cloister of your chest. Do not insist
on fetching stamps today; the greeting cards
can wait. Your boots are made to slip on
all that ice, gnarled as a scoffing lip. Maybe
she means to go indoors and pull
that soup from the cupboard. Ease out of
those jeans that feel like a corset choking
your thighs. Whom are you rushing and
scurrying for? The ones who love you
are patient. Better to rise as a rosy bulb,
a colt shaking off its frosty mane.

Appraisal

Thumbing through an old diary,
I come upon the question: *Is grief*

a measure of goodness? The query
sucks my ribs in tight, and I

wonder: the value of the rubies
of grieving that drip from

my fingers in ropes. Reading on,
I see I meant funerals, the grieving

of a person that takes place
in their wake. *Is the grief poured*

over a person a measure of their
goodness? is what I meant.

But I like this other reading,
the question it poses: could all this

grief mean goodness? Refusal
to drown out the pet's shocking

death? Refusal to shut out the
world and its roiling, ever-present

loss? Even when a thousand sources
snarl, *Stop being so damn sensitive?*

I imagine placing it on a
scale, this pocketful of grief

gems. Having some appraiser
raise it to her eye, say, *Don't you know*

what this is worth?! Like those
episodes where someone's thrift

store painting is a long-lost
masterpiece. I know this likely isn't

how God works, but
what a downy thought.

That an appraiser might gather
up all this blood and say,

Congratulations.
You kept your heart soft.

I Sort My Things Into Boxes

Things missed:

The exact spot at the dining table where I used to sit, where the light would filter through the tree in our neighbor's yard — a ginkgo tree, the leaves gold as buttercups — and do homework, or talk to a friend on the phone, or pet the cat. That exact spot, with that exact light. The light filtered, as if the glare of the sun with its full force would incinerate something, would reduce it to ash, and so, modestly, the tree sheltered me. Like a parent covering a child's eyes at the scary part of the movie.

Things not missed:

Sitting in that exact spot, veins coursing with adrenaline, wondering when you would be home.

Things missed:

The exact shade of turquoise we painted the bedroom, the one you let me pick, the color I saw when I would turn my head to the left to soothe the ache in my shoulder — the one you liked to make fun of, remember? — and again, the light: the way the light would filter in sometimes and make patterns on the wall, little angel scat of shimmers. The way the cat would curl into me, tuck under my left arm, the way she burrowed into the crook of me, almost spiral-shaped, and dream there.

Things not missed:

Watching the sun set against that wall, the spackled light growing dimmer, as I imagined you growing drunker and drunker at the house party up the road. Hearing you stumble in at 12, 1, 2, 3, or not at all. Hearing you stumble in or not stumble in — which, would you say, was worse?

Things missed:

Strangely, the struggle, the adamant struggle, to get away from you. It sharpened me like a whittler's knife. I was jagged; I knew my purpose. *You don't have to be so sharp,* you once said. But oh, believe me, I do. You can't coax the knife from the hand of a woman while pointing a knife at her throat. You can't turn a knife woman into a flower with petal guts crusting your boots. *You don't have to be so sharp* — is that so? Then let me just cleave my own head. This is what you got so wrong about me. I am no sacrifice. No sacrificial lamb.

Things not missed:

The coldness in your eye that could make breath visible, turn the whole living room blue. Your snort and your scoff as I pleaded for mercy, compassion, a little warmth. What I do not miss is me as a match girl: conjuring beautiful fantasies, freezing to death in the snow.

Things missed:

The version of the world I believed in before knowing such things could happen to me. The belief that although we did not have trust, we shared a kind of respect. It was like when my house got robbed as a child — the burglars just came in and took things. I can't get that version of the universe back, the one before I saw my father cry. The one where home felt like a safe place, the one where the locks do their job. I can't get that version of the universe back, where I think that even if I am not loved, I will merit a kind of respect. I can't get that back now. I wake up, still searching. This is the thing I miss most. The cat, the table, the light, the blue wall, the faith. That world. That faith.

The Selkie Agrees to an Interview

When you came onto land in woman form, what were
you hoping to do?

The moon was as full as a prophecy that night. I had wanted
to hear her aura sing.

When the man snuck up on you, didn't you sense him?
Didn't you sense his footfall?

The leaves were shivering. Aspen seashell whisper. I had closed
my eyes to better see.

You shed your seal coat there on a rock, had you not?
Had you really thought that through?

I liked the pattern my human-hand made, pressed against the
stars.

When the man approached, he took your fur robe?
Concealed it deep in his satchel?

He told me I was better off. He blamed it on magpies or
thieves.

How did you come to be this man's wife?

My weeping was pearls that spilled from my fingers. He laced
them on a string.

What was the wedding like?

Sullen. Sour. I cried in the cake when he brought out his flask and chased all the guests away.

How was your married life?

Picture two palms stitched to the window, flanking a faint mist of breath.

Why did you stay that way?

I could not find the exit. I knew I was missing something vital. I could not remember what.

How did you come to find your seal skin?

He had gone drinking with his friends. I saw it there, a sliver, beneath our mattress. I suspect, now, he rubbed it to his cheek at night.

How did you react?

I wept and wept. Pearls scattered across floorboards. I did not pick them up.

What did he find once you were gone?

My wedding ring pierced with a dagger. My white dress cut to ribbons. I carved a set of eyes in the mirror's wood frame so he would know the gods had been watching.

And did he follow you?

Of course not. The coward.

WHAT DID YOU DO THEN?

I dove back into the waves, fur thick, and swam, and swam, and swam.

DID YOU EVER LOOK BACK?

Now and then. Eventually.

WHAT DO YOU SEE WHEN YOU DO?

A thin line of smoke from the chimney. A rusted, misused gate. A well-trod path to the local bar. No circle of breath at the pane.

DID YOU LOVE HIM?

When wandering, lost in a forest, one might love any seeming guide, even a wolf.

DID YOU LOVE HIM? OUR LISTENERS WANT TO KNOW.

Like a deer might love an oncoming headlight. Transfixed, wide-eyed, feet firm.

WHAT IS LIFE LIKE NOW?

I paddle where starlight meets dark waves. I listen to the moon in my own heart.

WHAT WOULD YOU SAY YOU'VE LEARNED FROM ALL THIS?

My life is a creature not found in any book. One not easily described.

Do you have any advice for other selkies?

Our power lies in our transformations. Bless your story. Let it evolve.

Marina

Not to be morbid, but this is the beach
where I want my ashes scattered when I die.

Years ago, I came here longing for what,
despite my dents and scratches, I now hold.

Having somehow thread the needle between
Scylla and Charybdis, cut from the twine ball of fate,

woven like yarn through the minotaur's maze,
braided like ribbons into my own hair,

I gaze at the etching where I ached
by the fountain, standing on the cobblestone path.

Now, with your fingers lacing mine,
I could die here and not haunt these shores.

Pariah

It's true I didn't ask for this letterman
jacket draped over my shoulders.
Didn't ask for the scandalous life
events, the shrieking adjectives.

Who doesn't want to be the ingenue?
Who wants to be the pariah? And yet,
would you rather have had me walk through
that smashed glass for the rest of my days?

I will sit on the pier, dip my toes in the water,
watch all those gleaming stars shine.
Even with this jacket, red as a wound,
I can make a romance of the night.

Hot pink bubblegum shades on my head,
I am no one's cautionary tale. It's quiet
out here on the unforeseen path. There is
such infinite sky.

After the Phantom of the Opera

what is it about   the underside   of an opera house

       that calls me?

why do I yearn   to see   my own face

         in the lake   where no one swims?

my phantom,   you were all candlelit there,

    and I,   your supplicating student.

an apprentice of darkness,   a protégé

      denying my own need.

why did I go to you   time and again?

dancing your   sonata?

      what fascination kept me

watching your face like a blanched stormfront?

        what clouds would roll over you,

           stirring up trouble.

all I can say is,   like a good pupil,

I couldn't look away.

I wanted to see what mercury   would do,

let loose from the thermometer.

          wanted to see   what tune would play

from those empty, agonized hands.

     like birds fluttering   against shutters.

I wanted to see them   break through.

          I wanted to see them   against the sky,

     a siren song   in blue.

*

to deny you   would be to deny   some part

of this wandering   pitch heart.

     to deny that heart   would be to declare

my reflection not my own.

it's true I have an opera house

          pulsing in this sternum.

     it's true it has catacombs   inside.

it's true the   red-mouthed   thing in me

respects the same in you.   chaos.   a little

                    chaos.

but what you did not see,   what you couldn't

          echo   was that

I've got this well   of tenderness   in me

          with a bucket

that goes all the way down.

                    into the fountain of the earth, I mean.

          it pulls up

the cleanest water   you have ever known.

          and I use that spring   to water things

          that could never grow

below floorboards.   I use it to bloom things

          that part their petals

like lips   and issue   sweet breath.

          this is what you were missing

when insisting we live in shadow.

this is what   you were parching when

you claimed water was for the weak.

*

so, my phantom,   this is our discrepancy.

not our shared hunger   for tornadoes in throats.

not our shared wonder

for closing our eyes   and falling backward

through night

into night.

it's that I would never   drop chandeliers

or menace frightened page girls.

would never   polish another's   voice

just to see my own grin in its gleam.

would never   pose as an angel

while leering behind a mirror.

I just have   too much sun in me.

so you can keep   the drowning.

I know better now than to think that

a candle won't shine in the day.

Part Three
PRISM

Circumpolar

According to the Roman legend of Ursa Major and Ursa Minor, the bear constellations, the goddess Juno transformed a human woman named Callisto into a bear because she was jealous of her beauty. When Callisto's son Arcas shot an arrow at the bear, unaware that it was his mother, the god Jupiter deflected the attack and transformed Arcas into a bear as well. He placed the mother and son in the sky, where they would be safe from Juno's wrath. Still, not to be outdone, Juno ordered the god Oceanus to never let the constellations dip their feet in the cool waters of the sea. Some say this is why Ursa Major and Ursa Minor are what we call circumpolar stars — stars that never set below the horizon.

To wander the skies,
we callous our starlight.

Our paws pad the back
of the North Wind.

We dream inside
the Aurora Borealis,

bright seeds curled
inside folding quilts of blue.

We remember fur, wet
noses snuffling earth

and stone and dew. We remember
fish, clean flash and rainbowing,

bitten in grass, along stream,
in dark cave. Back, before that,

we remember dancing
on human feet with human legs.

We remember toes prickled cold
by fresh rivers, our skin

dappled netlike with sun. Callouses
washed smooth as glass.

Our bodies, now,
are made of stars.

We walk and are the sky.
We glance at oceans,

hear turquoise roaring.
Hear the seashells sing.

Dip and rise, my child.
Continue in our circle.

We see but may not reach.

Kitchen Scene

In the old brick museum, behind
a pane of glass, cookie cutters
sit still and silent. There are four
of them, cut in the shape of card suits:

diamond, spade, club, and heart.
Their ridged silver edges would have
made ruffled cookies, each the size
of your palm. I can almost see the

hand of the ghostly last user on the
knobbed green handles, a shadow.
Most likely, they would have been
used by a woman, or women and

women before her. An heirloom
passed down by multiple hands,
landing here now, so quiet, so clean.
And I wonder, like the cards

we draw from a deck, what fate
did these phantom bakers pull?
To the last cookie maker: was your
partner kind or cruel? What odds

did you stack yourself against?
Did you look down at someone,
brush flour from her cheek,
and say, *Here, we make our own luck?*

I wish for you sweetness, the softness
of batter, the grin as you lick the
wood spoon's curve. I wish for you
warm dough, the snap of a fire, a cat

for your quilt as the snow drifts down.
I hope you drew all the luckiest hands,
that any who came in with ice on their boots
found it melted before your hearth's heat.

Inheritance

I take myself out to lunch, trying to find the line between
mellow and *depressed.* Both can have sinuous piano soundtracks.
Both can charcoal-sketch similar self-portraits: a woman

alone in rain. On the TV with no sound above the doorway
where waitresses balance platters of food, a daughter pines
for her grandmother's wedding dress, locked away in storage

somewhere. The matriarch won't crack the safe open, though.
She wears her secrets like a cross. The plot won't say either:
why the young one is found wanting, deemed unworthy

of the gown. In the restaurant, a server sets down the special.
In the film reel of memory spiraling behind me, a man grits
his teeth in fury at my tears, deeming them frivolous,

accessories with no taste. As if I suctioned them there
with spirit gum, an actress pinning crystals to her cheeks.
The odious melodrama of it. *What is the myth of my life,*

I ask the ether that hangs in the air like smoke.
You tell me, answers the surface of the soup that shimmies
my reflection, a mane-shaking beast. Rain falls down

unceasingly, and I can't tell whether this is calm or morose.
The televised fiancée pleads with her grandma, begging for
what she believes is hers. And don't we all want to know

that line? Don't we all hunger to throw wide that sealed
portal? To see the bodice lying there.
To hear, *It's been waiting for you.*

The Patron Saint of Dinosaurs

The robbers stole your pillowcase. *They must have*
used it as a sack, your father murmurs, holding you.

This, the first time you see him cry. Grandma's pearl ring
is gone. The armoire's jaw is busted, sideways, a cartoon bully

with stars around his head. This, your slackened, loosened
home. Records tilt, askew. The neighbors explain

they saw flashlights in the window. *We thought you were playing*
a game, they stammer. *We thought you were telling ghost stories.*

And what is a ghost story? What are its bones? Is this a
ghost story — retelling the glint of the pearl, the birds

on the painted armoire that lifted blue ribbons like blindfolds
coming off? Mom loves to retell the time you sat in a circle

with other preschoolers, confronted the tall guest speaker.
A paleontologist who told a child, *Dinosaurs didn't swim.*

How you raised your hand: *Um, plesiosaurus did.* The finned
beast with a swan's curved neck and rows of jutting fangs.

You idolized dinosaurs. Their cavernous skeletons. Notes on
things extinct. Your bedsheets were awash in them —

stitched tyrannosaurus rex, gold triceratops. Stegosaurus
with her spine, as thorned as parapets. Merlons, embrasures

alternating, echoing impregnable castle walls. But this is
a ghost story too: a dwelling that cannot be entered.

Romanticizing bone reptiles. The notion that pillowcases have
just one use: something easy to rest on.

The Harvest

The garden had been my idea. And really, out of all the things
we tried to grow — bell peppers, cucumbers, cantaloupe,
squash — the pumpkins fared the best. They bulged, heavy,

golden, and orange, swelling in the loam amid pastel, hairy
vines. The pumpkins were spectacular. Still, their verve
was no match for the Pacific Northwest, its dew creeping in

like a flurry of barnacles. Slowly, tenderly as fingers stroking
fur, the rot set in, a damp, spongy thing. Two of the pumpkins
were spirited off and knifed into jack-o-lanterns.

We rotated them to cover the specks of umber and decay. One
hunched round in the garden, still living, and dying, nursing
from vine. A silver drizzle coated the landscape

of our backyard as we sat inside with tea. We contemplated
the squirrel-gnawed squash, the peppers that never bloomed.
My father nodded toward the final pumpkin, the solitary crop

that had dodged October's scythe. The ritual was his idea.
We blamed it on the play. He was starring, at that time,
in a one-act sketch that took up the theme of the scapegoat.

In one scene, he was to simulate adorning a small, white goat
with trinkets and cloth, then symbolically painting the sins
of its village onto its body and setting it free.

Onstage, he would mime watching the creature fade
on the horizon, its bell clanging out the vanishing traces of
wrongdoings and remorse. *We should try it,* he said,

blowing steam from his cup. *The damned thing's rotting anyway.*
Intrigued by this macabre suggestion, I went to the yard
with the long, clean shears and tattered, mottled gloves.

Mist clung to our faces and hair as we sliced the pumpkin
free. Turning it over, we saw that indeed, the belly was soft
and gray with putrescence. I carried it in and we dried it off,

bathing it of its grime. Much of the shell was still firm and
shiny. It did not yield when we took our pens and pressed
the tips against it. My father and I wrote our sins

on the pumpkin, solemnly at first, then with rising hilarity,
laughter alternatingly mirthful and tin. I wrote the name
of the class in which I was slacking at college, squandering

good days. I wrote the name of the boy I liked, who had
done wrong unto me. My father wrote the names of things
he knew he should love but, in fact, wanted to break.

We wrote these things in black and blue, a network of error
and pride. Confession and braggadocio both. When we
were finished, we set the scapegoat at the top of the hill

below our backyard. Wordlessly, we shoved it rolling and
leered at its bumbling fall. Near the very bottom, it struck
a stone and shattered into pieces, a firework of sloppy seeds,

string, and lettered crust. The drizzle yawned to crackling rain
and washed the ink from our fingers.

The Vision

Only twice have I woken up crying.
The first was when I was very young —

I dreamt my mother died. The second
was in my late twenties — I dreamt my cat

Luna was large enough to ride.
Larger than a horse. Larger than a house.

I climbed on her fluffy back like a tiny
doll on a dragon's spine. Her warm hair

smelled of milk. Together, we pounced
over neighborhoods, her delicate paws

dodging fences. I clutched her fur,
so soft in my hands, and felt perfectly

safe. I think I am searching for this
all the time. When I woke up, my eyes

were streaming. Nothing could hurt her
or me, you see. The small, fragile body

elevated. That cradle, so sturdy and un-
attainable, it unscrewed my heart like a cork.

The Fish Ladder

In the basement of the Ballard Locks:
the fish viewing room, window to a
world of urgent churning. Salmon climb
the ladder of turquoise blue, struggling
to rivers where they hatched.

Granddad often brought us here
when we were young, usually on free
parking days. Down we would go
to the cavern of concrete with the
square portals cut in its walls.

We would watch them, hands gripping
the cold guardrail. Watch their silver
scales flash like sabers. Pushing against
the punishing tide. All wriggling muscle
and wide eyes.

Granddad would point at some, huge
bites gouged from the hulls of their
glittering flanks. Still, those salmon
would press on, determined. Even
with ribbons of flesh trailing from

the spot where a seal or sea lion fed.
How many times have I thought
of this lesson and wondered just what
he was imparting? This was a man
who was shouldering depression,

divorce, and unemployment in the
cavern of his heart, though we could
not see in its windows clearly.
Did they mirror him somehow,
those fish that leapt ahead, despite

their missing chunks? Or was it
for us? Little wide-eyed grandchildren,
unknowing of the many teeth that
might take bites from us? I have
salmon days sometimes, days

where I feel that the current
I exist in might dissolve me. But I
think of him pointing, saying softly
with his eyes: *Keep going. You are
more than what you've lost.*

Malocclusion

The kind of day where the void is gently
       etched onto the world, scraping the tops

of buses. There like shining water
       you could reach out and brush. It seeps

into everything: the pine trees, your
       new boots. As if you could silently

inhale and just never exhale again.
       Just drift into that rainbowy sheen.

We're sold the bill of goods that with age
       comes experience, that what doesn't

kill us makes us stronger. You want
       to believe this, suck it through a straw.

Take stock of your inventoried earnings.
       But what did it get you, that dog-eared

scar? That love that bit and chewed and
       nearly swallowed you? You listen to the

pop stars the industry lets age and notice
       all their songs get sadder. Richer and more

textured, wine instead of bubblegum.
       It feels like a closely guarded secret. That pain

doesn't automatically add up to insight.
       That wounds might not bleed rubies. That the jaws

might have left you punctured
        somehow. A bite askew, a stranger to yourself.

Any selkie worth her salt has things she cannot speak
        about, and things she cannot stop speaking about.

I know this because I sing, now,
        from the ocean. The aftermath is its own story.

Love Poem with a Splinter in its Paw

They say even if a campfire is doused in water,
beneath the cool ashes, an ember can still blaze,

can still ignite a sneaky flame. I suppose
I am something like that these days. A staring

contest with the opposite wall. A finger twirled
in long hair. I bought myself this nightgown

both to languish and seduce in. Garnet, with
lace at the ribs. Once, feeling shame for

my so-called stunted teenage ways, I tried
to read the Idaho Driver's Manual; only

I had to stop when I got to the line,
The gray hours of twilight and dawn are the most

dangerous times of the day. The cadence,
the lyrical gravity of it, the almost-waltz of its step.

I pictured some underpaid government intern,
slipping their yearning in between pages

on stop signs and livestock's right-of-way. This is why
I cannot be trusted with houseplants. This is why,

despite the kind of self I wish I were, the leaves all
curl and swoon off. In the bedsheets we share,

there is a splatter of purple. We put it there,
an accidental drizzle from a brush, which we used

to cover up damage. You call our home a sky box, and
it is: a solid, square-jawed rectangle, sandwiched

between footsteps and more footsteps. I pout and say I want
to move when the buzzer goes out or the skittish bugs

creep in. But secretly, this too is my domain. A tiny queen
with nail wraps and half-closed eyes. The purple splatter

is my favorite thing about this place. It radiates: a narrative,
a signature, a pledge. They say, of campfires,

If it's too hot to touch, it's too hot to leave. I want these
walls to singe my fingers, christen me with smoke.

dusk, happy hour

the city is an opal, windows
pink-swirled with clouds.

light catches in my friend's wine,
an amber firefly.

moons glint on her delicate fingers.
the past is a bird on the back

of my chair, pesky and sharp.
patchy feathers.

now and then it tries to bite
my ear like an almond.

i patiently swat it away.
the city is an opal tonight

and i don't want this
bastard to mottle its gleam.

streetlamps blur on.
our server brings a candle.

we laugh and ask for
dessert with two spoons.

it all still perches there.
the alcohol-breathed ribbings.

the unpleasant mark
on my neck from That Time.

memory thick
as a talon.

but the city is an opal.
i'm telling you. look.

even if that anguish flutters
just outside its aura,

it's rose enough to keep
death at bay.

What Holds

I wander through the boysenberries
looking for others' validation.
It always seems to be around
the next corner, elusive as a scent.
Something that cannot be stored
in the belly. It doesn't work like that.

I want to say something about
kintsugi, how the cracks in a vessel
are filled in with gold, how the
breakage can be made beautiful.
I think, though, most likely,
you've heard that one by now.

And so have I. So what do you do
when the metaphor offered
doesn't quite suffice? What do you do
to conjure new wisdom?
Why such a dearth of rituals?
Why such a dearth of roles?

A teacher once told me, *You've got
to let go of where you've been
to get to where you're going.*
You've got to let go of who
you've been to become who
you are. And in the event

that you liked who you were?
I suppose you can carry a piece
of her with you, the finger
bone of a saint. Move as a living

reliquary, emphasis on "living."
Transformation isn't easy: I know

you know. Anyone who says it is must
never have had to pop off their tail
from the teeth of a steel-jawed trap.
Must never have had to gnaw off a paw
and move through the woods like that.
Just remember, in all those clichés

about caterpillars' innards turning to goo
right before they become butterflies,
the cocoon was never a mistake.
What you might not know about
kintsugi is that not all the fractures
got there by accident. Sometimes

crafters hurl them down, an act of
artistic choice. Thank God creation
is not so simplistic as to sift lives into
only good or bad. Thank God the world
has all kinds of interesting shapes
that we might make.

Discovery

Light falls across the Roman ruins —
I am visiting my friend in France.

As her husband parks the car and we
all file out, I ask when she knew

she wanted to live here. We grew up
together, but she's lived away for

years — well over a decade, now.
I knew when I met him, she says,

nods toward her husband. He locks
the driver's door and she ambles

toward the ruins. *Wait,* I say, scrambling
through tall grass, wildflowers. *I thought*

you knew way before that. My friend
is meticulous, crafting her life

like an elegant, well-balanced
bouquet. *Oh no,* she says. *The plan*

was just one year. I met him,
and everything changed. She smiles,

amused, quickening her pace
as I clamor over gray walls,

dart under cracked archways.
You changed your course for love,

I cry, startled and elated.
Yes, she says, laughing. *Yes.*

I have known this spirit
since we were fourteen, and still,

there is more to learn, more pathways
to uncover. I trot to catch up to her,

yapping like a seagull, badgering
her lovingly, demanding more detail.

Around us, the ancient stones
are washed in golden hour,

half luminous with memory,
half cloaked in mystery.

Wild Caraway

Early morning, I look out an unfamiliar window,
jet-lagged, having come here to escape myself, perhaps.

Nothing in the streets but sun mist and birdsong, until
a young woman with blonde hair and black clothing

treads in platform shoes to the field beyond a fence,
one of those feral patches nobody has claimed.

The grass is knee-tall, thigh-tall. She moves like a specter.
Her loose-fitting garments billowing, slow sails.

She bends and gathers fistfuls of the roadside vegetation:
long, headstrong sheafs of green and wild caraway,

with its sprigs that conclude in small, white flowers.
My companion and I debate: *Is she weeding? Is she*

making a bouquet? We see her pause to examine one
bloom, and it's decided: she has plans for her haul.

Later, rain-drenched, we wandered into an apothecary's
shop, the kind of place I didn't know existed anymore:

herbs on the walls and the heavy scent of wood.
And like something from legend, the maiden of the feral field

was there, the bouquet of caraway beside her on the counter.
Of course she found her setting in a space like this.

The disparity between us inspired a longing that tucked
my hair behind my ear and whispered that if I keep trying

to make myself so palatable, I might risk suppressing
any flavor at all. All the things that make me good,

someone will object to. A weed is a weed
unless it's placed in a bouquet.

Anthropocene Love

In the plastic vat of salad greens,
a tiny yellow blossom. Gold petals
bright as spangled prom shoes.

I pluck the spiraled tendril
out from lettuce leaves
and hold it toward you. Say,

For you. I mean it as a joke,
but your face illuminates,
a Northern Light on the horizon.

And who ever said that boys don't
like flowers? You place it in tap water
and keep it for a week. Say you

are glad our dystopia comes
wrapped in suburbs, parks
we can walk to. Love, you're not

wrong. The first time we stayed up
all night talking tasting notes,
that day we had wandered the

aisles of a grocery store
swaddled in cellophane.
The ratchetted summer had shot

refrigeration; the market
just wasn't prepared. Faithfully
masked and holding your hand,

I reached past the clear tarps
to pull out a yogurt and
thought, *We may be living*

in end times. But still, O you
whose face I trace with my gaze
as if it were a sixth sense — still,

I would still butterfly-tongue
the nectar from this small
and improbable bloom.

Poem That Resists Being Put Into Words

something about you is light unfolding
into more layers of light.

sunbeam on the floor I roll in,
an open-bellied creature.

wearing the ring you gave me,
milkweed and jasmine in my hair.

I study you like a painting sometimes,
study the life we are weaving.

it's delicate, like spider silk.
invisible as breeze.

I could lean into it,
a summer camp trust fall,

and never stop feeling held.
I want to practice walking with

my eyes closed in the night,
to know I can navigate

only by touch
the hallways memorized.

the body has a knowing
that need not be named.

the trust fall is more
than its naming.

words fall short when it comes to you,
like lace on the back of a tiger.

imagine my frustration,
calling something like that a bride.

that doesn't come close
to its wildness.

doesn't come close
to its nerve.

catnip, a friend said, hearing me
speak of you: I, your willing feline.

overflow, a friend said, watching me
speak of you: I, your pouring cup.

at the center of all those curtains of light
is a lotus with petals unfurling.

step inside and listen to
the silk shift of its pulse.

Copse, Corpus, Clearing

cherry, mahogany

any tree you want, I promise
to grow in the cloud-shaded

garden of our shared yard.
you say the past is a rainstorm.

the puddles are running.
in potholes, small ducks stir

up ripples. your coat
slung over my arm.

linden, birch

whatever you want. just
name it, and I will sow it.

we huddled and watched
as the drops whispered down,

only I was a phantom. I could
not have been there. it is all

I can do now, seeds in my pockets,
seeds overflowing in my hands.

elm, fir

I will pat them in the soil.
water them with cupped palms.

catch what falls
from the bright sky.

guard this land like a sentry,
safekeep what blooms.

if, in fact, this doesn't let up for years,
no matter. to gaze is a small thing.

maple, ash

in the café, I dug my nails into
my flesh to keep from reaching

for you. had to bite my inner
lip to keep the words

from gushing out. when I open
my grip, the skin is marked:

little half-moons everywhere.
train cars on a starved track.

cypress, oak

or, not cars, but basins, vessels
you could write your name in.

call yourself vertigo, spinning sense
as you laugh at the top of a tree.

wind in your hair, all billowing,
a gale snatching our voices.

I am here now, no phantom. body raked
like the earth where we bury our hearts.

110

After Orpheus

So, Orpheus fails   to get the girl

          from the grasping jaws of Hades.

She died on their wedding day,

bitten by a serpent,   punished by a serpent

for her revelry, her song.

And down to the Underworld she went.

          Swallowed like a mouse down a gullet.

Against all odds, Orpheus followed,

playing his golden lyre,

          which moved the stony   King of the Dead

                    to release the blushing bride.

Her taffeta all in tatters.   Lips still painted   red.

The only catch is,   *Orpheus,*

you must not look back.

Keep her in your mind even when   *you can't see her.*

          Let her keep   her mysteries.

He could not accomplish this.

Too much for his heart.

He turned,   and with that,

the mist enveloped her;

roots dragged her backward   into the gloam.

Hades smirked, wrapped his cloak   around her.

As for Orpheus,   he kept on

climbing northward,   up and out

to where grasses bloomed green,

singing.

Lyre. Liar.

*

This is where the story   usually ends.

But what of Eurydice?

I'll tell you:

she sat on the damp cave floor   wedged between

stalagmites.   Hugging

her cream and white appliquéd knees,

                              flowing with organza,

to her chest adorned with pearls.

                    Abandoned

and knowing it.   Beads of dew already

clinging to the high heels   she'd chosen

in hopes of all-night dancing.   Pallor sinking in

          despite her rouged cheeks

as she absorbed her situation.

And far above ground,   in the field where she was

bitten,   a different part of her rose.

Don't ask me to explain it.   You know we all have

some parts in need of rescuing,   others that do

          the saving.

So the headstrong part of Eurydice rose.   She picked

herself up from the dirt.

Rubbed the snake bite with a bit of antiseptic.

      Brushed off the hem of her gown.

Tied the long skirt in a knot on her hip

for easier walking   and running.

       Then set off for the Underworld's mouth.

*

Day turned to night as she marched across wetlands,

     leaving her stilettos in a thicket of mud.

Calves caked in pond grime,   she read the

constellations   as orange filtered out of   cobalt skies.

At last, the earth yawned and a stairway led down.

Keeping her hand against the wall's clammy rock,

     she lowered herself to the cavern.

     Moved through a tunnel with no light in sight.

Droplets from the ceiling   plunked in small puddles,

the only sound that echoed with her breathing.

Eventually,   a pinprick of lavender

slowly expanded to a lantern.

The ferryman, Charon,   raised a bony wrist,

          lifted his candle to the girl's face.

And what   will you offer?

he purred beneath his hood,   eyeing

her necklace of rubies.   She unclasped and held it out,

          a red star in the gray fog.

He pocketed the gemstones and grimaced.

     Insufficient, he said.   *This won't*

fetch her back.   It won't even cover your fee.

So Eurydice linked her hands over her sternum

and sang for him,   long and clear.

The melody spiraled upward like ribbon,

          dissolving as she finished her song.

Gray eyes narrowed in the ferryman's skull,

     but she saw something flicker beneath them.

Get on, Charon muttered.   She stepped onto the vessel.

With his long oar, he parted the waves.

*

       Across the churning river,   Eurydice alighted

on the sandy shore   littered with ghosts.

Avoiding their pinchers   and squirting mouths,

she pressed on toward   a large door in the distance.

     Just as its wood knots   came into focus,

     a rumble went up from a corner.

The Underworld's three-headed dog, Cerberus,   lunged

between her and the portal.

Just what   do you think   you are doing,

    little brat?

the first of the three heads snarled.

You know it is hopeless,   the second head cackled.

    How dare you even try this?   barked the third.

Eurydice took off her sapphire bracelet,
laid it gently at the dog's feet.

The first of the heads took it up in his speared teeth;

the others craned their necks to behold it.

A fine start,   the second head said.   *But no. Not enough.*

The first head gobbled it down.

All three monster maws started salivating,

huge paws lumbering closer.

Eurydice raised a hand to halt them,

and offered a song once again.

This one shimmered like fireworks,

cascading down in bright streams,

then fizzing on the ground to silence.

The dog's six ears stayed cocked

as she plucked a stray ghost   from her petticoat lace.

Six eyes stayed on her   as four paws moved,

then curled beneath the body, at rest.

She clutched the cold door handles and pulled.

*

Hades sat on his throne,   radiant and terrible,

beautiful and ominous as a solar eclipse.

          Why   have you come here?   the ruler asked,

robes shifting like quicksilver,   like moonlight.

I have come to bring myself home, said Eurydice.

It was not my time. I cannot stay here.

Hades beckoned,   and out from behind a velvet curtain

stepped the   other Eurydice,   eyes downcast.

          She was, he said, *abandoned here. She may not be*

          what you remember.

Nevertheless, Eurydice answered, *she is mine. She is my own heart.*

She sang softly, notes pooling up like crocuses,

          until her quiet double met her gaze.

          He tried to solve her like   a riddle,

          murmured Hades.   *That is why he lost her.*

Eurydice shrugged. *I am not him. Her depths are safe with me.*

          And what about that? Hades pointed to her gold ring.

Keep it, she said. *It belongs here,*   *with you.*

She tugged the band off   and placed it on the table

       alongside pomegranates and wine.

       You wish to go? Hades asked the dead Eurydice.

She nodded,   then handed him her ring too,

which he added to his pocket watch chain

alongside others,   the girls saw.

Hundreds   of others.

       The queen, Persephone, led the quiet Eurydice

           down from the dais

and linked the girls' hands.

              Before   you go,   she said,

     and took off her earrings,

affixing them to one of each girl's ears.   A pair

of hardened pomegranate seeds.

To remind you of where   you have been,   she said, gesturing to

          the Land of the Dead.

And to remind you of

each other, she added,   tracing their cheeks.

   Go now, and remember

that you are like sea tides: *helpless and helper*

   surfacing together

as needed. *As called upon by need.*

The girls brushed their earrings,

curtseyed to the king and queen,

  and headed for the exit hand in hand.

*

They move as one through the palace courtyard,

  Cerberus stirring up tiny dust devils

with the thunderous thumping of his tail as they pass.

On the shore, they see Charon's sturdy boat;

  he waves as they approach.

But the ghosts have been riled by the furious notion

  of a lost soul returning to life.

They rear on their hind legs as the girls pick up speed,

claw at the dead one's ballgown.

You are shameless, they bellow,   hurling clumps of sand.

You were forsaken. Act like it.

The quiet one shudders.   Her footsteps slow.

Charon urgently beckons.

Eurydice tightens her grip on her twin.   *Don't listen.*

They'll eat you if they catch you.

She sings a song like a winter quilt

that wraps around them both.

The dead one's brows ease.   They keep on   running.

You are defeated, the ghosts screech with bile.

You are unwanted. Unchosen.

The girls leap onto the poleman's craft

and the living Eurydice changes the tune.

She sings a song that flares like a comet,

sending the ghosts careening.

We're almost there,   she says to the quiet one,

who crouches

            and anchors her head in her hands.

*

All that remains is the tunnel out.   But this is single-file.

The living Eurydice leads the way,   as she must.

        This is the order of the Underworld.

        The dead must follow, unseen.

The passage is long and narrow and steep.

                        Rock walls the only guide.

The living Eurydice starts to climb,

sure she will not look back.

No footsteps can be heard behind.

No matter.   She has complete faith.

        Then again —

She pictures her counterpart   cradling her head on the ship.

        She wouldn't go down   that easily,

                                right?

Fear gallops forward   in horrible pointe shoes,

          pirouetting all around her mind.

Knocking over vases of roses.

          She mustn't look back. But maybe   a glance?

Just   to catch a glimpse   of her shadow?

The living Eurydice closes her eyes   and sweats

                    and starts to turn.

But before she can look,   she hears a soft voice

          coming from the quiet one's lips.

The dead one is singing.

                    The living one is singing.

Of course.   This is

                    a duet.

          Calling   and answering,

assuring each other   that they are both there,

still climbing.   That they are both devoted

          to the climb.

Stepping over slippery stones,

     dodging puddles,   they slowly advance,

          inch by inch.

The cave mouth appears in the mist-laden distance,

like a coin at the bottom of a fountain.

     The living Eurydice bursts into daylight.

She does not look back,

just hums a few notes,   and the dead Eurydice

     harmonizes.

Soon, both women   are standing in the sun.

Color returns to the pale one's limbs

as her blood resumes its beat.

     The two embrace. As their pulses

synchronize,   in a flash,

they rejoin into one form.

     She touches her earrings,   set in both ears now.

She touches her lips,   warm with music.

*

On her walk back through the fields,

she rests against a tree.

A pomegranate drops at her bare feet.

Splitting open, it reveals   a tiny scroll,

stamped with Persephone's seal.

Eurydice unfurls it.   The scent of spring flowers,

and letters scrawled in red ink:

And what did you find in the dark, my dear?

What did you find in the deep?

Notes

Versions of the tale of Bluebeard that helped inspire "After Bluebeard" include "Blue Beard" by Charles Perrault and "The Bloody Chamber" by Angela Carter.

Sources consulted for "Shears" include *BBC News*' "NZ's Famous Sheep Gets TV Haircut" and *The Sydney Morning Herald*'s "Shrek the Sheep has Close Shave on Ice."

The video game referenced in "Darling" is *Life Quest* by Big Fish Games.

The address to the heart in "Making Luck" is inspired by Mary Oliver's "Summer Morning."

In "Offering," the fable mentioned tells of a scorpion who asks a frog to carry him across a river. The frog worries that the scorpion will sting him, but the scorpion insists he will not, saying that doing so would mean they would both drown. Satisfied, the frog agrees to carry him. In the middle of the river, the scorpion stings the frog. As they begin to sink, the frog asks why the scorpion did it. The scorpion answers with some version of, "I'm sorry. I had to. It's in my nature."

"After the Phantom of the Opera" is inspired by the musical *The Phantom of the Opera* by Andrew Lloyd Webber, Charles Hart, and Richard Stilgoe, which was inspired by the novel of the same title by Gaston Leroux.

The italicized portions of "Love Poem with a Splinter in its Paw" are from the Idaho Driver's Handbook and smokey-bear.com's "Campfire Rules."

The myths of Callisto and Orpheus are based on various versions found online.

Acknowledgments

Grateful acknowledgment is offered to the editors of the following publications in which these poems first appeared, some in earlier forms and under earlier titles:

- *4Culture: Poetry in Public*: "Home Again"
- *Blood Orange Review*: "Darling"
- *I Sing the Salmon Home: Poems from Washington State* (Empty Bowl, 2023): "The Fish Ladder"
- *Isotrope Literary Journal*: "Sundown"
- *Eunoia Review*: "Wild Caraway"
- *Gulf Stream Magazine*: "The Selkie Agrees to an Interview"
- *Lit Shark*: "Ecology," "Appraisal," and "Anthropocene Love"
- *Persephone Literary Magazine*: "After Orpheus"
- *POETICS: Water — Life & Death* (Bainbridge Island Press, 2024): "Inheritance"
- *Potomac Review*: "Hematite Heart"
- *Reedy Branch Review*: "The Vision"
- *Scavengers Literary Magazine:* "Murals"
- *Shō Poetry Journal*: "Love Poem with a Splinter in its Paw"
- *Spirit: A Compendium of Esoteric Poetry* (White Stag Press, 2023): "Marina"
- *Spry Literary Journal*: "The Harvest"
- *SWWIM*: "Copse, Corpus, Clearing"
- *The Broken City*: "Oyster's Clutch"

- *#WATERTOME* (White Stag Press, 2020): "Impasse"
- *Writing the Self-Elegy: The Past is Not Disappearing Ink* (University of Illinois Press, 2023): "Alchemy," "Falling Three Ways," and "The Patron Saint of Dinosaurs"

The following poems first appeared in the chapbook *Simple Magic* (Ghost City Press, 2022): "egg tarts," "Making Luck," "Joy Spell," "Shears," and "Imagine."

In addition, grateful acknowledgment is offered to the curators of the following museum and gallery exhibits in which these poems first appeared, some in earlier forms:

- *Embracing the Dark* (VALA, 2024-2025): "Origin Story of the Oracle," "Burnout," and "Solstice"
- *Redmond Historical Society Poetry Showcase* (Redmond Historical Society, 2023): "Kitchen Scene"
- *Tall Tales* (Boise Art Museum, 2016): "Circumpolar"

Also, thank you to The Rice Place and Gröndal's House for providing inspiring spaces in which to work on these poems.

* * *

A book is never born in a vacuum, and I'm immensely grateful to each and every person who offered encouragement, feedback, and support along the way. Special thanks to my mom, Diane, as well as my friends Hannah, Shilo, Jason, Laura, Lynne, Alisa, Jana, Ryan, Abby, Jillian, Bryn, Jennifer, and Carl for reading and commenting on earlier drafts of these poems. Thank you to Carl, in particular, for observing that many of the poems were asking about the value of sensitivity — this became something of a guiding light for the collection.

In addition, thank you to Wendy, Jenny, Jenn, Hillary, Lisa, Lessie, Stefanie, Cristina, Kyle, Bailey, Danielle, Betsy, Ray, Courtney, Amber, Sonia, Fara, Claire, Vanessa, Jeannine, Erika, Kristine, John, Remy, Tess, Mical, May, Nazia, Rachel, Will, Ember, Dave, Susie, Sarah, Gwen, Julie, BriAnne, my dad David, and all the other loved ones who helped keep the fire of writing lit within me, even (and especially) when things seemed foggy. As always, to everyone who has offered a kind word to me or my writing along the way, please know that I am grateful.

Thank you to Alex for bringing me home, for being the "ever after" on the other side of all the aftermath. I look forward to writing many new chapters with you.

Finally, thank you to Diana and Kels for bringing this book into the world. Your care and insight polished it greatly, and I am truly thankful.

About the Author

Catherine Broadwall is a poet and memoirist from the Pacific Northwest. In addition to *Aftermath*, she is the author of *Water Spell* (Cornerstone Press, 2025), *Fulgurite* (Cornerstone Press, 2023), *Shelter in Place* (Spuyten Duyvil, 2019), and other collections. Her writing has appeared in *Bellingham Review, Colorado Review, Mid-American Review*, and other journals. She was the winner of the 2023 Paula Svonkin Creative Arts Award and the 2020 COG Poetry Award, as well as a finalist for the poetry categories of the 2021 Mississippi Review Prize and 2021 Pinch Literary Awards. She holds an MFA from New England College and a Ph.D. from Western Michigan University.

Her website is www.catherinebroadwall.com.